Copyright © 2020 J.K.Simon

All rights reserved. No part of this publication may be reproduced or distributed in any form or by any means, or stored in a database or retrieval system, without the prior written permission of the author, except where permitted by law.

Legal & Disclaimer

The information contained in this book is not designed to replace or take the place of any form of medication or professional medical advice. The information in this book has been provided for educational and entertainment purposes only.

The information contained in this book has been compiled from sources deemed reliable, and it is accurate to the best of the Author's knowledge. However, the Author cannot guarantee its accuracy and validity so cannot be held liable for any errors or omissions. Changes are periodically made to this book. You must consult your doctor or get professional medical advice before using any of the suggested remedies, techniques, or information in this book.

Upon using the information contained in this book, you agree to hold harmless the Author from and against any damages, costs and expenses, including any legal fees, potentially resulting from the application of any of the information provided by this guide. This disclaimer applies to any damages or injury caused by the use and application, whether directly or indirectly, of any advice or information presented, whether for breach of contract, tort, negligence, personal injury, criminal intent, or under any other cause of action.

You agree to accept all the risks of using the information presented inside this book. You need to consult a professional medical practitioner in order to ensure you are both able & healthy enough to participate in this program.

Contents

Table of Contents

Introduction 5
A Description of Success *5*
The Key to Success *6*
Golden Key #1: Interactive guides, practical steps, and key takeaways from the Description and Keys to Success. *7*

Chapter 1 8
The Habits of Successful People *8*
Golden Key #2: Interactive guides, practical steps, and key takeaways from the Habits of Successful People. *10*

Chapter 2 11
Secret Habits of High-Performance Leaders *11*
Golden Key #3: Interactive guides, practical steps, and key takeaways from the Secret Habits of High-Performance Leaders *13*

Chapter 3 14
High-Performing Leaders take Self-Care *14*
Golden Key #4: Interactive guides, practical steps, and key takeaways from the Secret Habits of High-Performance Leaders *16*

Chapter 4 17
Impact of Positive Mindset & Meditation on your life *17*
Golden Key #5: Interactive guides, practical steps, and key takeaways from the Impact of Positive Mindset & Meditation on your life *20*

Chapter 5 21
Meditation is an integral part of Success – The Law of Attraction *21*
Golden Key #6: Interactive guides, practical steps, and key takeaways from Meditation as an integral part of Success *23*

Chapter 6 24
Practical Examples *24*

Golden Key #7: Interactive guides, practical steps, and key takeaways from Practical Examples.. 28

Chapter 7 29
   Successful People Embrace Failure *29*

Chapter 8 31
   The Science of Failure *31*

Chapter 9 33
   The Fear of Failure *33*

Chapter 10 35
   Know and Understand your Competitors and Opponents................ *35*

Chapter 11 39
   Technology and Meditation.. *39*

Conclusion 41

Check Out Other Books 43

References 45

Introduction
A Description of Success

It is challenging to pinpoint what success is as the meaning of success differs for each. Some of you may find that success is in having the latest model cars, a good reputation, a large house at the beach, and others find success living a fulfilled, contented life with their loved ones. Here are a few traits that define a successful person:

Eight Common Traits of the most successful people in the world:

Passion – They do it for love

Success is driven by passion. If you love what you do, the way to success is already crossed. No amount of money can replace the love you have for what you do.

A niche

The love you have for something – the passion – will inevitably lead to your niche. Our niche is where you will perform at your optimum.

Failure is an art

The best part of being passionate and having a niche is that you do not fear failure. Failures just become part of the fabric of learning.

New ideas

Failure often leads to new and innovative ideas. However, the successful person never stops thinking of new ideas.

They stretch their comfort zones

Failure and new ideas are often related to the stretching of comfort zones. Successful people, though, will generally make it a habit of stretching their comfort zones.

They seek to learn continually

By stretching your comfort zone, you are bound to learn new things. This means that you will learn continuously, but it is also necessary to continually learn new things.

They provide value to others

Sharing with others is an essential outlet for success. It adds value to the lives of others as well as your own life.

They work hard and play hard.

Successful people have crafted the art of working hard but have also made the effort of balancing through the art of relaxation.

Here are some quotes on success from famous individuals to motivate you on this journey:

> Bruce Lee: "Always be yourself, have faith in yourself, do not go out and look for a successful personality and duplicate it."
>
> Dwayne Johnson: "Success isn't always about greatness. It's all about consistency. Consistent hard work leads to success. Greatness will come."
>
> Wayne Huizenga: "Some people dream of success, while other people get up every morning and make it happen."

The Key to Success
Techniques of Success

Commitment is fundamental to the success of any individual. Most often, passion will follow commitment. However, it is still necessary to make commitments the key to your daily life, especially if you are working on specific projects.

Even though you have to set goals, it is important not to worry about the results. Every step of the committed journey is a learning opportunity. Thus, the focus should be on learning and not on the results.

The truth is that the journey of commitment and learning can sometimes be difficult; it is essential to have fun.

It is vital to keep the creativity going so that the process and progress of your success do not stagnate. You should, therefore, make every effort to keep your thoughts on the task.

Creativity stimulates the imagination, and this is vital for success. Our imagination occupies much of our thoughts. We can, therefore, drive our thoughts to create an image that leads to our success.

To drive you forward to success, it is a vital part of the journey to challenge yourself. You can use your creativity to challenge yourself as well.

Staying focused, setting goals for each day, and having fun at the same time, will help keep the distractions away.

To achieve the set goals, it is often necessary to work independently. This will ensure that your daily goals are met and that you complete projects on time.

If you work independently, you will need to plan your day as well. By planning your day, you have the ability then to assess your progress regularly.

The most important key to success is to protect yourself from burnout. The aspect of having fun along the journey is, therefore, a vital part (Stasiulionyte 2019).

Golden Key #1: Interactive guides, practical steps, and key takeaways from the Description and Keys to Success.

Define success.

Find out how you view and define success?

What do you regard as being "successful?"

Is it money, power, or a fulfilled life?

Once you have defined success:

Determine the path to achieve it.

Think positively to help you challenge setbacks

Avoid negative thinking that will cloud your plans.

Live in gratitude.

Be thankful for everything in your life, mostly if you worked hard for it.

Success is a personal journey.

Follow your own path.

Don't compare yourself to others.

Don't let circumstances hamper your journey.

Your life consists of the good and bad choices you make

Therefore, love your life no matter what.

Change is the only constant in our lives.

Finally, if you need to make changes, grab the opportunity to do so with both hands; you are the only one who can succeed in your life. Other people can be part of your success and happiness, but it is up to you to make it happen. Remember, life is a journey, and you may be successful today, but not tomorrow. So learn from each mistake and go find your success. Good luck on your journey (White, 2019).

Chapter 1

The Habits of Successful People

The question is always: How does one become successful? As mentioned in the introduction, success needs to be habitual. The reference is specifically to how we ought to stretch our comfort zones. As Leon Ho, founder, and CEO of Lifehack, says, it is all about forming habits. He also refers to the power of positive thinking; in that, we can create circumstances that will help us accomplish our desired success. Furthermore, the desire to succeed is part of the willingness to commit and not give up when difficulties arise (lifehack.org/879930/make-things-happen).

Habits of Successful People

Consistent habits are an integral part of the success of successful people. Successful people know this and stick to them. A good habit of creating a positive outcome for the day is to have an early start in the morning. The early morning start is often highlighted by a daily and consistent routine, which may include meditation. It may also include time to journalize your thoughts, plan the day, or sketch out goals for the day. The key is to do this consistently every day, without fail.

A successful person develops these habits over time, and it becomes entrenched in their lives. These habits spill over into their entire life and impact the qualities mentioned before – self-esteem, self-confidence, and self-image. Depending on your definition of success – that is, how you perceive success – this would be a success story in itself. There are many habits of successful people, but we can mention a few here:

We have already mentioned that a good habit is to rise early. This habit resonates in most written texts. There is a famous saying, "the early bird catches the worm."

Apart from journaling and planning, successful people also read extensively to educate themselves on matters at hand or for future purposes. People in finance rise early to know how the financial world early each morning by reading the newspapers.

Previously I have mentioned that I read some books that inspired me and could refer to them as my inspiration or mentors. However, nothing can replace a real person as a coach or mentor. I also mentioned how friends could inspire you to greater heights. Thus to be successful, you could also find a coach or mentor that would inspire and guide you to reach greater heights in your life.

Two scenarios are played out in the next ten chapters, and that is in the context of a successful business person and a professional athlete performing at peak level in their respective professions, so focus on these target groups when reading the next chapters.

Meditation is not necessarily always about clearing the mind, but it can also be a matter of focusing the mind. Many successful people would use their morning time to focus on specific ideas and thoughts on solving problems.

Another great habit of a successful person is the fact that they exercise. Exercising is also a means to keep you refreshed, stay focused, and have great health benefits as well.

You mustn't compare yourself with others. The successful person forms the habit of setting his or her own goals and follows them resolutely. No two people are the same, and you must set goals that you can achieve.

Getting enough sleep is very important. It allows you to rest, feel refreshed, and have an active mind. This corresponds with being positive as well. Thus, going to bed at a decent hour slots in with the fact that you need to rise early.

Each day has specific hours, and in planning the day, the successful person does not waste any time. It is essential not to waste time, because as the saying goes: "time is money."

Most importantly, a successful person does not "put all your eggs in one basket." Diversifying is a habit that successful people have discovered over many years. Most successful people associated with the stock exchange in the world have portfolios with various income streams.

Most of the habits in this list are related to the success of a financial nature, but one can apply these to most successful people (Ward 2017).

The Characteristics of a Successful Person

In defining a successful person's characteristics, one must look at the things they do in daily life.

As mentioned before, when you make mistakes, you have to forgive yourself and move on. That is in the context of positive thinking. If you achieve this, it is so much easier to forgive others' mistakes. A trait of a successful person is to be able to forgive, forget, and move on. This means getting rid of or emptying your mind of all negative emotions and refilling it with a positive mindset. A positive attitude will reflect positive energy and affect your business or professional club environment positively as well.

Building on the positivity, you should compliment people and analyze their work rather than to criticize. The difference between studying someone and criticism is that analyzing evaluates rather than giving negative input.

In light of the above, the successful person would wish others only the best, as they would want others to succeed as well.

In the context of where a failure occurs, a successful person would take full responsibility for the incident instead of blaming others. It is about learning from one's failures and building a new strategy for future reference.

The habits that they establish in their daily lives; successful people will always follow through on it. They do this as a matter of principle.

What is vital for a successful person is that they always know what they intend to be. Some reinvent themselves constantly (Ho 2020).

Golden Key #2: Interactive guides, practical steps, and key takeaways from the Habits of Successful People.

This chapter outlined the kind of habits you can use to create a successful life. Evaluate your circumstances and create your own habits using this as your guide. Some of these habits are:

- A good habit is to rise early. As the saying goes: "the early bird catches the worm."
- Educate yourself on matters at hand or for future purposes.
- Find a mentor that would inspire you to greater heights.
- Meditate to clear and focus the mind.
- Exercise daily for focus and health.
- Do not compare yourself with others. Set your own goals and follow them resolutely.
- Getting enough sleep is an important habit.
- Do not waste any time, because as the saying goes: "time is money."
- Make diversifying a habit by not "putting all your eggs in one basket."

Chapter 2
Secret Habits of High-Performance Leaders

The Inner Man

When an airplane experiences an emergency, oxygen masks are released from the overhead compartments. Even though it seems selfish, a mother, for example, should first attach it to her own face before she attends to her children. This is important because she needs to be prepared and protected to assist them. This relates to the secret habits of a high-performance leader. The inner man is important for such a leader to be consistent and perform at high levels.

The secret habits of high-performance leaders involve focus and effort. Their focus is on the inner man. Many often see this as egotistical, but it is a matter of investing in you first. You cannot be a strong leader if you are weak inside. This is clearly seen in the previous reference to the kind of person a leader should be (see Chapter 1). If you look at the example at the beginning of this chapter, you can also see that you cannot help others if you are not strong enough, especially on the inside – that is, building strong positive emotions ("What's the Secret Habit of High Performing Leaders?" 2018).

Some athletes have strong belief systems and build their leadership on the spiritual strength they gain from it. Their inner strength comes from their faith, and they build it even further by getting together as a team, for example. The Fijian rugby sevens team is known for getting together to develop their relationships and celebrate their victories. This motivates leadership on all levels in the team as well. Some people regard the Fijian rugby sevens players as superheroes. This is an excellent example of how a strong inner core can drive one to success (Leamer 2016). Hence, what is the Inner Man or the Inner Core we are talking about here? Well, you should find out in the next few chapters.

Athletes often become motivational speakers and leaders because they build a strong inner core. Not so long ago, Fortune Magazine highlighted Serena Williams (2018), LeBron James (2017), and Ohio Governor John Kasich as part of a list of most outstanding world leaders. They base the strength of their inner core on the following:

They create their personal philosophy that is true to them only. Once they have established their philosophy, they stick to it. This is what guides a positive mindset and the setting of end goals.

The goals are set within a plan and the map to achieve those goals. This sets the stage for them to stay emotionally and mentally healthy.

Furthermore, they focus on learning from mistakes and the expectant growth from it (Hayes 2018).

Mastering the Inner Man

By mentioning athletes as high-performance leaders, I want to draw your attention to their success because this is our focal point. The focus is also on the secrets of how they achieve this success. One example slots in with what I mentioned earlier, the mindset of discomfort – that is, that we should stretch our comfort zones. According to LeBron James's championship teammate in the NBA, Richard Jefferson, LeBron "never wants to feel comfortable." Thus, it means that he wants to push himself to the extreme to perform at extraordinary levels. It is about never being comfortable with the ordinary and mundane. It is always about pushing yourself to the next outstanding level.

These achievements are possible through the mastery of your emotions and your mind-"the Inner Man" There cannot be any place for negative thoughts or feelings. The mentally strong and high-performance leaders have mastered the skill of taking control of their bodies, minds, emotions, and their spirits – that is, "the Inner Man." They do this through:

The constant search for improvement

Maintain the ability to perform at high levels in all circumstances.

Pushing them to higher performance because they do say, "You are only as good as your last performance."

The fact that being average is not acceptable.

That means that you need to be extraordinary, and that takes hard work and effort.

Creating mechanisms for de-stressing and coping with pressure.

Ideal Performance State (IPS)

The Ideal Performance State (IPS) is limited to athletes and corporate executives who have the same desire to perform. They should do this with the express desire to perform at an optimum level under all circumstances whilst taking care of themselves as athletes do. Loehr and Schwartz highlight that high-performance leaders and athletes take care of their spirit, mind, body, and emotions – 'The Inner Man."

All high-performance leaders should perform at their best to reach an ideal performance state. This state is indicated by exceptional and consistent performance. It often means that the body is trained for an athlete and can perform at maximum without any pressure. This allows for fun and relaxation whilst being in the midst of competition. This can be duplicated in the boardroom where the business person can apply the same principles. This will give them the same state of confidence, focus, and relaxation to perform at an optimum level, even under extreme pressure.

Thus, a high-performance leader carves out a way toward success by going beyond the usual standards. A well-known high-performance coach, Brendon Burchard, indicated that these leaders do so over a long period as they develop and grow, never satisfied with the ordinary. Performing as a high-performance leader takes commitment in the long term. Most important of all, the leader has to take care of his or her well-being.

Golden Key #3: Interactive guides, practical steps, and key takeaways from the Secret Habits of High-Performance Leaders

High-performance leaders have personal habits that are easy to follow.

You need only to focus and put in the effort.

Once it is a habit, it becomes valuable to you

You can apply it to all circumstances in life.

Focus on:

- Your inner person helps you build a strong core from which to operate.
- Remember, this does not happen overnight. It is a long-term mastery of the inner person.
- It is about building your spirit, mind, body, and emotions.
- With a strong inner core, you are bound to push yourself to more challenging heights to achieve your goals.
- It is about achieving the Ideal Performance State (IPS) and maintaining it as a lifelong commitment.

Chapter 3
High-Performing Leaders take Self-Care

It is an essential factor for the high-performance leader to take care of their self. I have referred to this in Chapter 2 under the heading of the Inner Man. One can refer to several aspects here to emphasize this essential factor. The most important aspects to remember are that the high-performance leader should ensure that he or she takes care of their emotional state, their mental state-the Inner Man, their spiritual state, and their health. Even though this seems repetitive, it is vital for the leader to keep in mind if they wish to reach an Ideal Performance State (IPS). As stated before as well, it is important to ignore any references to being egocentric as your health and well-being are more important (Loehr and Schwartz 2018).

Taking Care of the Body

An American basketball player for the Los Angeles Lakers, LeBron James is an excellent athlete who is highly admired for his skills as well as his leadership around managing himself and others around him. We don't see him as egocentric, as one of his former teammates, Mike Miller, suggested that he invests in his body physically, mentally, emotionally, and spiritually – "The Inner Man." He allows for physical recovery through conditioning of his physical body and having proper rest.

For more than a decade, he has been using advanced rest techniques. LeBron's resting techniques include sleeping adequately and listening to his body. He drinks a lot of water, invests in quality time with his family, and uses music to unwind. During free throws, he conserves energy by walking to the other side of the court after a rebound instead of sprinting. Mental toughness training is a priority to him to ensure that his Inner Man is fit. He engages in his emotional well-being by taking part in community activities and spiritual sessions. This is all part of his powerful anti-stress ritual. By taking care of his body and health, he ensures that he can continue to perform over a long period.

Your exercises need not be as elaborate as LeBron's, but you could do simple exercises in your own context. For example, you could find time during the day to do breathing exercises, short meditations, simple yoga exercises, disconnect from your electronics, and focus inwardly for a few moments.

The corporate leader also means similar activities as this athlete who invests in electro-stimulation, massages, and ice baths. Even though these might not be the activities you wish to participate in as a corporate leader, there are alternative techniques to keep your body in top-notch shape to achieve a high-performance state.

Taking Care of the Mind

Furthermore, a high-performance leader can only perform at their best with a healthy mental attitude. I will cover the Power of Positive Thinking in Chapter 4, which can only be reiterated here as part of the high-performance leader's arsenal to take care of the mind or "the Inner Man."

It is essential to understand that the athlete's competitive edge is not limited to physical performance but has a vital mental aspect to it. Most athletes can overcome grave challenges by being mentally prepared. This is an excellent lesson for corporate and other leaders. A well-prepared mental state will allow you to know what is going on around you at all times. This is another page from LeBron's booklet of high-performance. He concentrates his mind on every part of the game and reiterates that his preparation for a game is ten percent (10%) physical and ninety percent (90%) mental.

Taking Care of the Spirit

Preparing your mental state and physical state for any leadership activity is an excellent part of your daily routine, as LeBron's stress management ritual shows us.

However, as we have also seen with our reference to the Fijian rugby sevens players, the spiritual aspect of one's life needs attention as well. Many athletes had experienced times when spiritual intervention helped them throughout the long seasons like the annual World Rugby Sevens Series played in ten different countries worldwide with varying zones of time. The physical body is subject to wear and tear; the body clock has to adjust and acclimatize and become subject to injury, fatigue, and sickness. They can suffer from jet lag, and on-field or off-field misconduct and other disciplinary issues can put a strain on the spirit.

It is essential to understand that spiritual intervention is based on whatever your belief system is. You can pray to your God to help you with your performance in whatever aspect of your daily activity. However, being spiritually attuned to your God does not exclude the aspects that we have discussed thus far. Your spirit is part of the other aspects of preparation for outstanding performance. A meditative heart and spirit will keep you calm and secure in the midst of challenges.

Taking Care of the Emotions

Most high-performance leaders will, at times, face very stressful situations. Corporate and sports leaders also have to perform in very competitive environments, leading to very stressful situations. The executive branch of companies is expected to perform at high-performance levels, which can lead to stress and illnesses.

This is the reason why many companies advise stress-management techniques to their executives. However, the individual should take care of their stress levels on his or her own as well. If these stress levels are not managed well, it can lead to negative emotions that can impact their performance and, ultimately, the overall individual or company performance. This requires some serious actions like investing in the time, money, and resources and getting yourself prepared emotionally, spiritually, physically, and mentally daily.

Golden Key #4: *Interactive guides, practical steps, and key takeaways from the Secret Habits of High-Performance Leaders*

Stressful and competitive environments are everywhere, but it can be considerably more for the corporate environment where executives need to be in an ideal performance state most of the time. The same applies to professional athletes and sportspeople.

1. Perform at an optimum level consistently over a more extended time by taking care of yourself.

2. To achieve longevity in oneself over a more extended period, it is highly recommended that you take all the necessary steps in taking care of your body, mental being, spiritual, and emotional state.

Taking care of yourself requires practical steps such as:

- Investing in time, money, and other resources
- Commit long-term to achieve the end result, which is a success.
- There are no short cuts.
- Trust this process.

By following these steps, you would not only live a happier life, but you will also see an increase in your ideal performance state. More importantly, you will see an increase in your earning power and be a role model for others to follow (Loehr and Schwartz 2018).

Chapter 4
Impact of Positive Mindset & Meditation on your life

The previous discussions here touched on various ways how one can improve one's mental state, especially as a successful leader. Examples of how professional athletes improve their mental capacity through meditation to perform at the highest level and achieve success remain a top secret to this day. The majority of people do not know this secret. Here, I referenced the outcome of positive thinking for being an effective leader. However, it is vital to give some idea of how this mental strength develops. It is about training the "Inner Man" that can be achieved aside from merely changing the mind to think differently.

One can define success in different ways, and there are various factors to achieve such success. The success of an athlete differs from that of a corporate executive as their accomplishments are highly individualized. One aspect is, however, the binding factor that a positive attitude does contribute to success.

As discussed in the other chapters here as well, success is achieved by different factors such as positive thinking, which is a matter of unlocking the Inner Man. It is worthwhile to investigate how you can achieve this goal. One way of doing this is through meditation. Most religions, such as Buddhism, Hinduism, and Christianity (to name a few), encourage their followers to meditate. Meditation will encourage you to do a few things differently. The following aspects do not teach you how to meditate only but also guide you to becoming a better leader through meditation.

These aspects, as an outcome of meditation, will allow you to:

Control your anger: If you are confronted with a situation that you disagree with, you would be able to draw on the calm moments of your mind. This will allow you to step back, look at, and assess the situation before drawing conclusions and reacting. This is a good outcome for individuals involved in contact sports such as Basketball, Rugby League and Rugby Union, National Football League (NFL or American Football), Soccer, MMA, Boxing, and Wrestling (to name just a few) and non-contact sport such as Cricket, Golf, and Tennis.

Avoid unnecessary confrontation: confrontation is often unavoidable, especially when your leadership is challenged. Meditation teaches one to go to a quiet place in the mind, and it is constructive when you are confronted with an irate employee or client. By remaining cool, calm, and collected, you will be in a position to de-escalate any confrontation. This too is a good outcome for individuals involved in contact sports such as Basketball, Rugby League and Rugby Union, National Football League (NFL or American Football), Soccer, MMA, Boxing, and

Wrestling (to name just a few) and non-contact sport such as Cricket, Golf, and Tennis.

Have a grateful disposition or gratitude: Meditation teaches one to reflect on the positive, which often includes recent successes. This pleasant experience leads to gratefulness or being in gratitude. By nurturing this gratefulness, you will continue to have interactions and situations that contribute to your experience. This will add to your happiness and overall well-being, as well. Just being thankful to your God for surviving the COVID-19 pandemic is one example of being grateful.

Forgive others: This is an aspect touched on earlier in this book but is extremely important because your meditation can be marred by un-forgiveness. If you hold a grudge against anyone, you will find that it interferes with your meditation and the positive outcome you desire from it. It comes with emotional baggage that affects your mental state that, in turn, affects the Inner Man.

A Positive Mindset

One might ask what contribution positive thinking makes to the success of a person. As part of a life strategy called the Law of Attraction, positive thinking helps to achieve a life of success. The "Law" states that we attract what we think about and focus on in our minds and hearts. Thus, you might want to think more positively to be successful because positive thinking works on the notions of "likes attract likes." We might ask the question: How can I achieve it? When you meditate and think positively, you release positive energy, which results in attracting positive things to affect your life. For example, you may mediate over 12 months, spending a minimum of 15 minutes per day about a promotion from your current role, and eventually, you get promoted.

The power of positivity helps you in seeing the world differently. It opens more possibilities before you and enables you to discover your key to success. It broadens your mind in many ways and helps you to manifest positive emotions such as contentment, gratitude, joy, and love.

To be successful, you must positively think that will allow you to expect the best and get the desired effects. The desired result is a positive mindset that helps you to seek health, happiness, and a positive outcome regardless of your situation.

There is evidence that many successful people use positive thinking as the key to success. Therefore, it is possible that the power of positive thinking may change your personal and professional life. It is incredibly valuable in difficult situations. A successful person can use positive thinking to their advantage, such as in the list below:

By having a positive mindset, you have the advantage of de-stressing and have a much calmer disposition.

A calmer person is much happier and, as a result, lives a healthier life as well.

This can lead to a better self-image that leads to self-confidence and better self-esteem. It also leads to confidence in your abilities. The more this occurs, the more successful you become.

Self-confidence motivates you to make good choices and decisions.

If you are positive, you can discover what you are good at. Knowing what your best skills are, feeds your positive mindset. It is the best route to a successful life.

To accomplish a positive mind, you would need some techniques. Below is a list of how you can create a positive attitude:

- You should start each day on a positive note. Find a quiet time and spend 15 minutes each day meditating on what you want in life.
- Humor and good thoughts are good ways of starting your day.
- Mistakes are not bad happenings, but they offer opportunities to learn.
- Don't dwell on the mistakes, but forgive yourself and move on as soon as possible.
- Positive friends and mentors help in creating a positive mindset as well as a positive lifestyle.

It is important to note that negative thinking can debilitate your day-to-day operations. Negative emotions, such as worrying or getting angry, will create tense situations. A negative mindset narrows and focuses your thoughts, which causes you to function at a minimum level. You are, therefore, unable to find solutions to problems and other challenging scenarios in your day.

If, for example, a lion chases you, your only thought is to run. You focus on running because your only concern is your life. The fear makes you forget to attempt other things such as climbing a tree or grabbing a stick. There is no chance of thinking positively under such conditions. This applies to real-life scenarios as well. Positive thinking can assist you in achieving more and finding solutions to your problems.

Finding a Positive Mindset

Here are a few of the books that had a significant influence on my life. Please read them to see how others can influence one's life. I would venture to say that these authors are my mentors.

> *On Thoughts*
>
> This has been the most important book of my life. It was written in 1910 and has guided me for 45 years. *As A Man Thinketh* by James Allen
>
> *On Bliss*
>
> Follow your Bliss by Joseph Campbell. It will show you ways to find your bliss and live a fulfilled life
>
> *Think and Grow Rich* by Napoleon Hill. Another book, which was written in 1937 that changed my life. It showed me how to apply the knowledge from As A Man Thinketh.
>
> *The Millionaire Next Door* by Thomas J. Stanley

Golden Key #5: Interactive guides, practical steps, and key takeaways from the Impact of Positive Mindset & Meditation on your life

1. Meditation is the key: You should make meditation an actionable part of your professional life

2. This is true, whether you are an employee, professional sports personality, or high-performance leaders such as CEO, Managing Directors, Board Directors, Governors, Member of Parliament, State Ministers including the Prime Ministers and Presidents.

3. Meditation ensures that you develop a habit of clear positive thinking.

4. It reinforces positive energy each day.

5. It will help you control your tension or negative energy such as anger

6. It will provide you with a tool to de-escalate adverse events such as conflict or confrontation.

7. It leads to a grateful heart as well as give you the motivation to forgive others (Wuest 2018).

Chapter 5
Meditation is an integral part of Success – The Law of Attraction

Many different tools can be used that can contribute to your success. We mentioned tools such as journaling, planning, and exercise, as well as meditation. It plays a huge role in obtaining a positive outlook on life (the power of positive thinking). We highlighted meditation in the previous chapter, but here are some practical steps on how to integrate meditation into your daily routine to ensure success (Kotobalavu). However, you must remember that meditation is only one part of striving toward success.

> Inspirational Quote:
>
> "You will see it when you believe it" — Wayne Dwyer

Step 1: ASK for what you want

One way of overcoming difficulties in life and the professional working environment is to dig deep within. The simple routine of daily meditation can achieve this. Meditation helps you with visualization, especially if you need specific successes such as a new job or even material possessions. As we noted before, professional athletes meditate and even pray to achieve their goals.

The key to successful meditation is to clear the mind and be concise in what you want to accomplish. For example, if you desire a new job, a new vehicle, or a new house, you should visualize this during your meditation sessions.

This is an undeniable part of the Law of Attraction, and you need to be clear so that it might manifest and attract you to what you want and desire in life. Unclear goals will attract unclear results, bringing confusion into your life.

Steve Harvey, stand-up comedian, motivational speaker, and popular TV host, emphasizes the need to write down your goals so you can read and meditate on them each morning. Writing down your goals is an integral part of meditation. There are literally thousands of thoughts that filter through your mind each day. In order to be specific and capture the thoughts that are vital to your success, you need to write them down. If you do not do this, these thoughts will get lost; therefore, it is vital to make it a habit to write them down.

Once it becomes a habit, it will not be a chore but become a daily fun exercise. This habit allows you to make your requests, let them free, much like you would leave a balloon, and know that you do not have to repeat the same requests. Once you have your request set down, you can move onto the next step, which is asking. Yes, Ask is like making an order through a drive-in fast food like KFC or McDonalds. When you ask, be specific to what you want in life. Maybe you have been living in your car for the last 3 years and want a new house or a new job. Well, you should list that down and ask. Or you want to achieve personal success in your respective sporting or business career. Things like "I want to be the Most Valuable Player (MVP) this year" or win an individual Grand Slam title this year.

Step 2: BELIEVE that you have received

Believing that your requests will materialize is simply the act of dreaming as you did when you were a child. It is a matter of imagining that you have received what you asked for, even if you have not received it as yet. This is also the visualization part of meditation.

Each day, during your meditation, close your eyes. This act makes it easy to imagine, especially if you have already reached a state of sheer relaxation, and your thoughts are focused.

Music plays a vital role in helping one meditate. A particular genre of music and even specific lyrics can move you to an emotional trance that will motivate the visualization of your goals.

By repeating the same visualizations, over time, the conscious mind transfers your visualizations to your subconscious. This leads to the belief that you have already received what you asked for.

It is essential to stay focused on the positive manifestations you want in your life. What we have reiterated throughout is that the law of attraction can only work in a climate of positive thinking. The same applies here when you meditate and visualize.

Step 3: RECEIVE what you asked for

When you meditate and visualize your desire, it is vital to create the emotions that accompany this.

This could be an easy task, especially if you create a strong visualization in step 2. However, the emotions you create here could also enhance the visualization and the belief that you are receiving your desire.

Some of these emotions include happiness, excitement, elation, and delight.

You could also add physical effects such as pumping the air with your fist, lifting your arms in victory, or shouting out. Just remember this is a meditation period, so the physical assertion of joy can be shown towards the end of your meditation.

All you have to do is to ensure that your visualization is as creative as possible. Perhaps you could turn your meditation period into a movie with your choice's necessary emotions and soundtrack. You can place all the desires of your heart into this movie. As you keep replaying the movie, the subconscious takes over and allows you to use all available resources to achieve success.

Golden Key #6: Interactive guides, practical steps, and key takeaways from Meditation as an integral part of Success

Meditation is an integral part of success, and most successful people and elite athletes knowingly or unknowingly perform some form of meditation in their professional working life. If you follow the three steps suggested here, you are tapping into your wealth of untapped endless resources in your subconscious mind. The conscious mind is part of the physical world and relates to the five senses: sight, hearing, smell, taste, and touch and connects to the physical world we live in. However, the subconscious mind is the Inner Man that is referred to throughout this book. As part of the Law of Attraction principle, ask and believe, and you shall receive it.

- Ask for a job, money, vehicle, relationship, and wealth as these things are already meant for you.
- With meditation, it is stored in your sub-conscious world
- Commit and make an effort to find a quiet place and ask for it.
- Do this with a positive mindset
- Meditate for 15 minutes every week and work towards receiving it.
- Meditation is part of unlocking the enormous, endless wealth stored in your sub-conscious mind.
- It relieves stress and tension.
- It improves balance in your physical or conscious world, and keeps you calm, increases awareness and relaxation.

A relaxed mind helps to increase your intellect as well as your creativity. It improves your ability to learn and also improves your memory.

By reducing anxiety and depression, you will also lead a much happier and productive life. This will affect your relationships and personal well-being, increase your energy, help you heal, age slower, and above all, and help you reach your goals quicker. More importantly, meditation with a positive mindset helps tap into the subconscious mind, trigger positive responses to your requests, and allow your body to be charged with positive (neutrons) vibes. When your mind and body are positively charged, you will attract positive people; receive positive feedback, which will impact your life positively.

Chapter 6
Practical Examples

Hard Work Equals Success

Success does not fall into your lap. It comes with hard work. Some are born with the proverbial "silver spoon in the mouth," but for most people, you have to put in the time and hard work to achieve success.

LeBron James: In Chapter 2, LeBron James featured prominently, and it is worth mentioning him here again as he is a prime example of what it means to work hard to be successful. Even though he is an extremely talented player who will mark his 17th season in the NBA by the end of 2020, he works hard to be the top player and improve his skills and talents daily.

Cameroon Smith: Athletes, in general, become successful because of hard work put in and not just because they are talented. The Australian National Rugby League (NRL) competition is a very tough competition, for example. An athlete such as Cameroon Smith of the Melbourne Storms Rugby League Club has to work exceptionally hard to stay at the top of his game for over 19 seasons and 430 professional games. Over this period, his hard work involved investing in his personal and family time, money, and other resources. He trained and trained hard and used customized training methods on his mental, emotional, and physical conditioning (mainly resting and recovering) to prepare for each game.

The All Blacks is a New Zealand rugby team that has dominated the rugby world for many years. Much of their success is based on simple hard work. The ethic of hard work is instilled in the players at a very young age. It starts at school and is cultivated right up to the eventual acceptance into the national team. The simple reason is: It is both talent and hard work.

Inspirational Quote:

"I don't believe in magic. I believe in hard work." — Richie McCaw, former Blacks Captain.

The success of the All Blacks Rugby team is a combination of many factors, and the key among them are:

"Warrior mindset" associated with Maori Culture. This Maori Culture "Warrior mindset" begins at an early age. For a typical New Zealander, rugby starts in kindergarten. Kids are groomed culturally, physically, and mentally right from a young age. The pursuit of athletic and sports excellence is part of their high school and college culture and education.

When the player reaches the national level, he or she is so conditioned both physically and mentally with the warrior mindset that combined with talent; they turn into world champions, thus, achieving success. Hard work and foundation put in place by the New Zealand Rugby Union (NZRU) system over the years contribute to the ongoing success of the All Black organizational structure at the top level in New Zealand.

The governing body – NZRU, is in control of all aspects of the sport, including the top super rugby clubs such as the Crusaders, Highlanders, Hurricanes, Chiefs, and the Blues. This implies that the NZRU and the All Black management can significantly influence how the clubs play at the top level right down to the grassroots level. Compared to other big nations, the Australian and English rugby union systems are quite different. Furthermore, rugby is everything in New Zealand. It is part of their culture and tradition and boys growing up aspire to wear the All Blacks jersey. In Australia and England, though, rugby is generally geared more towards meeting their respective clubs' financial needs than achieving consistent success at the highest level.

The Right Attitude for Success

Part of Cameroon Smith's and LeBron James's preparation and training involves preparing the mind: the Inner Man. As they age, they spend 90% of their time on mental preparation and 10% on the physical body. For them to be successful and achieve longevity in the game, they have the right attitude, which requires a 90/10 ratio.

One of the reasons why most of the athletes such as Lionel Messi (aged 33), LeBron James (36), and Tom Brady (at 43), can still play in their respective sports disciplines is that they combine both mental and physical aspects in their training. Even though players are allowed to play at an older age, it would still depend on their mindset, hence the 90/10 ratio in training.

When asked about the difference between the two, Ken Norton, the heavyweight boxer, explained why Mohammed Ali beat him. He explained that Ali could defeat anyone with his mentality. Even though he was physically able to beat his opponents, his mental state made him successful.

The New Zealand rugby team has strong ties with Maori Culture. This warrior attitude drives the team to be as successful as they were for so many years.

One could reflect on the Fijian rugby sevens team as their spiritual commitment drives their attitude. They are known for getting together and praying before they engage in a game and do the same afterward, which results in consistent success in bigger tournaments like the World Rugby Sevens Series.

Commitment and Trust toward Lifelong Success

Most of the examples mentioned here are also concurrent with lifelong commitment and trust toward success.

Cameroon Smith, for example, has a very long track record of success. So far, he has played 430 professional rugby league games over 19 seasons. It is a historic world-record since 1891 when the rugby league was born in England and adopted in Australia as well. It comes down to his personnel commitment to his diet, commitment to his preparation, training methods, and continuous work with his coaches and other experts to improve his game in every game of his career.

The examples of athletes such as Cameron Smith, Lionel Messi, LeBron James, Tom Brady, and the New Zealand rugby team give you the idea of what it means to have a lifelong commitment to hard work. With the right attitude, invest in your physical, emotional, mental self towards a goal and believe in yourself (in your natural talent) to achieve long term success in the professional arena.

Golden Key #7: Interactive guides, practical steps, and key takeaways from Practical Examples

The practical examples here show that highly successful people make sacrifices, make commitments, and raise their expectations to higher standards all the time. As examples point out, success does not come easily or appear magically. It takes hard work and effort; you need to have the right mindset and attitude, as well as the commitment (personal and financial) to reach your goals to achieve success.

The athletes mentioned here appear to have positive attitudes, and one would assume that they are happy with what they have accomplished. It is for this reason that they inspire us. We often think that successful people quickly achieve success, but practically this is not the case and no longer the truth. To be successful, therefore, it is essential to:

List down clear goals. For example, 'I aim to play 80 or 90 minutes of football in each game or, I aim to achieve a 30% profit margin, after analyzing the sales numbers using the Pareto principle of 80/20 rule in business.'

Work hard with a commitment to attend training, pre-season training, weekly training, strength, and conditioning, and to get adequate rest and recovery time from injury. Eat the right kind of food, nutrients, and supplements as well as attend community, social, and well-being sessions. Your own club for professional athletes should be able to provide you with these facilities.

Professional businessmen or women could attend boot camps, yoga, or Zumba. They could set aside a quiet time each week for spiritual and mental (meditation) sessions. For meditation and yoga, go to a quiet place and practice yoga and meditation for about 10 to 15 minutes each session. Remember to be clear about what you wanted, ask for it, and hard towards achieving it.

Invest in yourself by, for example, hiring external experts to advise you on how to improve your performance. Even if training is available overseas, make arrangements and take a trip to attend refresher courses.

Develop highly effective work habits: don't let anything go unattended or unchecked by reviewing your activities with your managers every week, continuously checking and monitoring progress. It is essential to pay attention to detail and remain ahead of the pack.

Develop a positive mental attitude that would lead to our happiness and success.

Your positive mental attitude leads to an optimistic mental and emotional state that produces positive results in your business and professional working life.

You should repeat this each day, each week, each month, and annually.

The examples allow you to see how success progresses and develops and how you, too, can achieve success by setting goals for yourself. You should start with a goal, set out a plan, and commit (personally and financially) to it. You should remember that these are, first off, long term goals and plans.

These athletes' success stories can be mirrored in your personal life, the corporate environment, and many other professional sports disciplines.

Inspirational Quote:

"Success is just the progressive realization of a worthy goal" – Earl Nightingale

A few bits of advice from a famous professional athlete (wrestling) and Hollywood actor, Dwayne Johnson: He said the following:

Create your own future – "Success at anything will always come down to this: Focus and Effort and we control both."

Gain perspective – "Think back five years ago. Think of where you are today. Think ahead five years and what you want to accomplish. Be unstoppable."

Be Relentless – "If something between you and your success – Move it. Never be denied."

Little habits acquired daily – "Success isn't overnight. It's when every day you get a little better than the day before. It all adds up."

Chapter 7
Successful People Embrace Failure

No matter who you are or which part of the planet you live on, failure is a part of life. Most successful business people stand by the rule that failure is an essential part of success. Perhaps one might want to refer to Michael Jordan as an example of the definition of failure. His expression of failure, if applied to any other environment, is very much part of success.

Michael Jordan clearly states that it is his failures that make him successful. He embraces failure even though the world only sees his success. It is essential to look at his entire career graph, see his failures, and understand that all of us fail at one point or another. It is all about embracing failure in order to succeed.

There many other successful people whom one might regard as failures today. One of the significant aspects is that most of them were regarded as failures, but we only strive to see their success. Another good example one could refer to here is Vera Wang. She failed at becoming an Olympic figure skater and a Vogue editor but became a very successful fashion designer. Perhaps the latter is also slotted in with what we mentioned before – that is, you need to find your niche. However, you can fail even within your niche, and it is a matter of embracing that and moving on as most successful people do.

In chapter one, we allowed you to think about what success means to you. This will determine how you will view and interpret failure, as well. That is because failure comes at different levels, particularly in light of where you are on the success ladder. After all, failure is an integral part of success.

Golden Key #8: Interactive guides, practical steps, and key takeaways from How Successful People Embrace Failure

Picture yourself and your team in the ocean. Success is the "iceberg" that you or your friends notice, visible to everyone. No one sees what happens underneath the deep ocean. They only see the visible part. This is precisely what Michael Jordan's example tells us. Nobody knows the risks you took, the number of failures you endured, the sacrifices, the hard work you put in every day, the focus and the persistence, and the goals you and your team set. They do not see the actions and small steps (work habits) you and your team take to achieve overall success. Knowing what lies beneath allows successful people to embrace failure because they know failure is an integral part of your success journey.

The success ladder affects the mindset and attitude toward failure. The higher up you are on the ladder, the more open you are to it, and the more likely you are to embrace it.

Successful people use failure as a lesson and to teach others how to overcome similar errors. Life coaches, high-performance coaches, and business mentors, for example, are highly skilled professionals that can guide you to overcome costly life mistakes. You should seek them out and engage them, as they are an investment as well.

Furthermore, embracing failure helps you change your attitude as well. If you look back on your own life or see your children, you will see how they lift themselves up after a failure. When a small child starts to walk, they often fall, but it does not prevent them from getting up and trying again.

As adults, we ought to adopt the same attitude when we fail to accomplish our goals.

Children also seek to learn new things and, in the process, often fail at it. This is the same attitude that adults should adopt. You do not always succeed at the first try; therefore, "If at first, you don't succeed, try and try again."

It takes courage to fail; hence, do not be discouraged when you fail.

Furthermore, by shifting out of your comfort zone, you are bound to fail. Therefore, an essential aspect of failure is not to be afraid to move out of your comfort zone and try new things.

Successful role model, Michael Jordan clearly stated that he was never afraid to fail. This is an attitude that would go a long way to allow you to accomplish success (Titaniumsuccess, 2019).

Chapter 8
The Science of Failure

One could perhaps give a short description of the science of failure like this: it is the fact that a person is open to criticism, not afraid of feedback, and unconcerned about getting it wrong. However, by assimilating all the points discussed so far, is that it takes courage, commitment, habit, and endurance to achieve this.

Some of the following will further expand on the science of failure:

Admitting that we are wrong

One of the most challenging things for most people is to admit that they are wrong.

When mistakes occur in a workplace, for example, people tend to deny the failure.

Most people would take credit for their successes but will not readily take credit for failure.

Failure is often credited to external factors rather than a personal failure.

It is vital to acquire the skill of admitting to errors (or mistakes) to learn from those instead of denying them. We have covered this aspect in previous chapters here as well.

Becoming a more generous person

A successful person will gain confidence and, as a result, become quite helpful to others. They feel the need to pass on their knowledge.

However, someone who fails will feel less confident in their abilities and will therefore become less helpful.

The key here is that generosity can be cultivated, especially if the person admits to being wrong. These people can then deliver products to others that are filtered and error-free.

Successful people share their failure

Those who admit their mistakes are often seeking out ways to make mistakes. As said before, it is a way of challenging yourself and learning from your mistakes. It is also a way of developing a better way of doing things. It leads to the leadership of sharing those mistakes and teaching others to take courage in admitting their mistakes.

A great example is Sara Blakely, who prided herself on starting her own business from scratch without any experience. She put it down to the fact that she was never afraid of failure, a trait that was instilled in her by her father.

Golden Key #9: Interactive guides, practical steps, and key takeaways from The Science of Failure

This aspect plays a vital role throughout the book. It is possibly an essential aspect of success. Some of the ways how one can learn from a mistake are by doing the following:

Failure is an integral part of success. Therefore, you should list your failures, learn from them, and make it your target to convert them into success. How? You can do this through continuous improvement in business processes. In the professional sporting arena, make sure to set your mind towards achieving the 1% in effort areas designated by the coaches in each game played.

Journaling is an excellent way of documenting your failures. This could also be part of the meditation exercise, as mentioned in Chapter 5. This process is a way of developing a debate with you to analyze and reach certain conclusions differently. You can do this as detailed as you wish to see how the mistake evolved and how it can be stopped in the future.

Once these are documented, it is easy to review the process and see whether you can find different or better solutions later.

The best part is that you can see these errors, how they occurred, and learn from them. Thus, you can also document your successes.

What is important here is that you can create several options and experiment with them to give you the desired outcome. Most coaches and mentors in businesses and the professional sporting industry use these methods. However, some life coaches, skilled coaches, and performance coaches use methods such as the 1% effort areas in each player and team members to improve their performance in every game played.

Failure, therefore, need not be a negative experience. The crux of the matter is to learn and grow (Cooper, 2020).

Chapter 9
The Fear of Failure

As said at the end of the previous chapter, failure need not be a negative experience. It should instead be a motivation to learn and grow. Apart from that, it can also be the motivation to step out of your comfort zone. In order to start on the journey to overcome the fear of failure, it is crucial to know and understand the factors that contribute to this fear.

The Meaning of the Fear of Failure

Everyone experiences failure differently, which means that each individual will understand the effects of fear differently. As with success, each person regards failure differently. Hence, you need to discover what you consider as a fear of failure.

For example, when you are confronted with a new task, you might experience certain symptoms that will indicate that you fear failure. Some of these are:

You hesitate to do the work and are reluctant to move forward. You may also avoid volunteering and participating in challenging tasks – that is, you would prefer to do more straightforward tasks.

Another clue is that you procrastinate as well as sabotage yourself by not following and meeting your goals.

Previous failure experiences often leave you with low morale, low self-esteem, and a lack of courage to attempt new ventures.

Your view is that you would not start something new if you cannot complete it with perfection. Thus, you might describe your fear of failure in this way.

Reasons for Fear of Failure

Earlier, we mentioned how Sara Blakely's father helped her to see failure in a positive light. If it were the opposite, she would have grown to despise failure. Therefore, negative input from an early age can lead individuals to regard failure as a negative part of life.

Individuals fear failure in light of experiences of the past as well. A traumatic experience can, for example, lead to low self-esteem and the lack of courage that is fertile ground for failure.

Failure to perform well at important tasks can cause reluctance to participate in new projects.

Golden Key #10: Interactive guides, practical steps, and key takeaways from The Fear of Failure

This booklet has given you many gems to learn from. It is also important that some things are repeated throughout. Examples of overcoming fear are similar to what we have touched on in other sections. Here are some of those examples once more:

You can analyze your situation and what the outcomes might be. As said before, a great way of doing this is by writing the fear down. By writing these fears down, you can document and create a visual presentation of the outcome's different scenarios. For example, if you fear or are not good at public speaking, you could join Toastmasters or become a community member such as a church, a member of a group that organizes public events or causes.

Most professional clubs have community and well-being programs throughout the season, which you should seriously think about getting involved with because it could improve your weaknesses, such as your emotional, mental, and psychological state. Lack of awareness increases fear of the unknown and therefore become a weakness. Try your level best to understand all aspects of your game, business, and your professional self and the wider community and stakeholders involved.

Here again, the power of positive thinking can be of great value. By making use of tools such as meditation, spiritual exercises (prayer or yoga), physical exercises, rest and recovery, healthy and balanced food and nutrient intake, planning, and journaling, provided here, you are bound to build your self-esteem, your self-confidence, and self-belief, and self-image to overcome the fear of failure.

Writing down and visually presenting the scenarios will help you look at the worst-case scenarios. By thinking through each case rationally, you will see that it might not be as bad as your negative thoughts indicated.

By mapping out the scenarios, you can create scenes that would include contingency plans. This is simply a replacement for potential failure. Knowing that you have a back door will help you overcome the fear of failure (The Mind Tools Content Team et al.).

Chapter 10
Know and Understand your Competitors and Opponents

Most businesses do not operate in isolation. We have also addressed you as an individual finding your niche, but it is equally important for a business or company to find a niche market. Finding this niche, however, does not secure or guarantee success. It is, therefore, important to find ways and means to achieve success in whatever form. Many business owners have discovered a way to succeed by applying the teachings of Sun Tzu's *"The Art of War."*

Gaining Understanding and Knowledge

Depending on your success definition, you need to employ some tools to help you achieve your goals. Your success is often defined as promoting, achieving your goals, being happy, and finding your niche. It is sometimes necessary to know and understand those who would compete against you and those who oppose you. In real terms, the "opponents" are not always individuals but can also be your own failures and everyday battles with various projects. Hence, a few things to be noted:

According to Tzu, it is important to know yourself. By knowing yourself, you would have the ability to make use of unconventional methods to achieve success. Barker makes the analogy of David and Goliath, where David slew Goliath with an unconventional weapon. You might not have the power and strength of a colleague, but you can use your experience and knowledge to achieve your goals.

Therefore, it is vital that you gain as much knowledge as to become competitive and achieve success as a result. Remember that knowledge comes from failure as well as successes. Your failures, for example, will teach you how to operate in a similar scenario specifically. You have also gained knowledge of your opponents and competitors through these experiences. This will give you the edge over them. As they say, "experience is the best teacher" in life.

Golden Key #11: Interactive guides, practical steps, and key takeaways from *Know and Understand your Competitors and Opponents*

The best way to apply the knowledge and understanding you have gained is by taking practical steps:

Preparation is the key to the successful execution of any game plan. You should make every effort to obtain as much in-depth information as possible (of yourself and that of your competitors) so that you are well prepared for any situation during game day or when you meet to discuss a business deal.

Know your yourself:

List your strengths, for example, work experience,

List your weaknesses such as your failures, for example, public speaking

List what opportunities are available; starting with the low hanging fruits that do not require any effort, for example, what you are good at (your talents).

Know your competitor:

Know their strengths by listing, for example, their work and play ethic, their player depths in such as the backs and forwards. Good players make use of technology and use experienced coaches. It is essential to have the inside scoop on these aspects.

List their weaknesses and failures, for example, their weaknesses in how they read the defense if they are using inexperienced coaches, inexperienced players, or inexperienced workers.

List opportunities available starting with the low hanging fruits that do not require any effort, for example, what they are good at that they can use to exploit your team. These include their talents or attacking flair, a good kicker, tall and heavy players that they can use to cause havoc in the aerial and lateral battle.

For example, if you are called for an interview, it is important to research the company and know as much as you can about them. The best way to do this is to call the company and speak to those who work there directly. In a professional team environment, always listen to the head coach and his coaching staff and not be afraid to ask questions. In a work environment, you should always listen to the supervisor or your immediate boss or the CEO. Why is this important? Because they will guide and impart knowledge (know-how) and lay out game plans to exploit opportunities for a single game, a single business working day, or the entire playing season. Most of this knowledge becomes part of your life, which is often referred to as your experience. An experienced person can use the acquired knowledge learned throughout his/her professional working life and use it repeatedly in another business, professional club, or simply to improve his life and that of others around him/her. Again remember "experience is the best teacher' in life.

The knowledge you obtain is also there to help you understand what might be in opposition to your ideas. This is one of the ideas from the pages of Sun Tzu – that you gather the information in order to "actively exploit and manipulate the assumptions of the other side" (Barker 2014).

You need to be confident, but you need to balance that with humility. Do not be over-confident when dealing with executives or leaders – that is, do not try to show off or that you know it all but humble yourself and always remember to give credit to others who help you succeed.

Many professional people employ the "Art of War" principles, especially coaches of teams and individual sports competing at the highest level, like the Olympic Games or professional matches. Today they use technology, making it simpler and faster to research opponents using real-time high definition video replays and sports science to improve and increase performance at the elite level.

Do you wonder what the secrets of the success of some of the top elite athletes are? Some sports personality like the Formula One champion, Lewis Hamilton, employs sports science research and engages high-performance experts and personal trainers such as Angela Cullen, an athletics speed expert to maximize his performance on the track. Professional sportspeople like Hamilton invest in high-level personal speed trainers and physiotherapists to compete at the highest level and have a competitive edge against other top competitors and eventually achieve success on the track.

As a professional athlete, businessperson, or politician, you should be gathering knowledge about your competitors and making commitments to invest in professional and expert help in personnel life. You should engage life coaches to be consistent and remain ahead of the pack. This will go a long way toward achieving long-term success and happiness. Here is a list of some experts:

- Personal, professional experts that you can reach out to:
- Physiotherapist
- High-Performance coach or manager
- Professional Skills coach
- Professional Business or investment advisors
- Professional Life coaches
- Professional Spiritual Coaches (Combination of Yoga, meditation, Prayer, Cultural expert)
- Professional Food and Nutrient coaches/experts
- Professional Talent Manager/ experts
- Medical Doctor
- An experienced Lawyer
- Professional Counsellors
- Sports Psychologist or Human Resources manager (Psychologist) for businesses
- A Political Strategist
- Professional Technology or Social Media Manager is a growing need by professional athletes and business for their social media platforms such as Facebook, Twitter, Instagram, and other platforms.

Inspirational Quote:

"If you know the enemy and know yourself, you need not fear the result of a hundred battles. If you know yourself but not the enemy, for every victory gained you will also suffer a defeat. If you know neither the enemy nor yourself, you will succumb in every battle." Sun Tzu, The Art of War (Barker 2014)

Chapter 11
Technology and Meditation

We are living in the age of technology, mainly the digital kind. We have noted here that LeBron James makes use of music to relax. This is possibly the most effective way to relax. In recent times, technology has developed at warp speed, so much that every person in the world could perhaps be connected to some form of technology in the future. Currently, we are connecting with laptops, desktops, digital television, tablets, and the most portable at this point, the mobile phone or "smartphones." These devices have become the go-to for most types of communication but it has also increased in the use by what Poindexter calls "mindful technology" (Poindexter 2018).

This meditation method is on the increase and, in particular, the Software Applications (Apps for short). Two of these Apps are quite famous and offer users a choice – they are called Headspace and Calm. These two are the most outstanding competitors, meaning, as we discussed here as well, it could lead to a better product as they push each other to create the next best product. But since 2019, Calm has been extending its content to include celebrity contributions. They are using relaxation music by Sabrina Carpenter, Moby, and Sigur Rós. They have also signed a three-year contract with LeBron James, who will offer "inspirational wisdom sessions" of ten minutes each. These messages would be constructive for meditation, stress relief, and relaxation.

Golden Key #12: Interactive guides, practical steps, and key takeaways from Technology and Meditation

We cannot escape technology, and it is improving each day. It dominates our lives today and into the future, so don't hesitate to use it to your advantage and achieve success. If we use Calm as an example, we will have several benefits and can ultimately achieve success:

Even if we suggested here previously that we could turn off our digital devices to find a meditation period in our day, we could use this digital option for our meditation on the flip side.

Just as you would go through your meditation manually – that is, have your written down text in front of you, play your music, and think positive thoughts, the App can do this all or you.

The App is beneficial as you answer several questions, and it will automatically personalize it for you. This is ideal, especially in your busy day-to-day schedule. The App gives you options for meditation guidance, breathing exercises, and music.

For those who need affirmations, what better than LeBron's motivational talks mostly lined up for the next three years. (Gonzalez 2019).

Conclusion

This book attempts to give you practical ideas and ways to become a successful person. There are many ways to gain and maintain a successful life, and this is only a fraction of it. Some of the methods include the following:

You can start by defining what you deem as success.

Realize that the way to success is a personal journey. This means that you should not compare yourself to others.

It is essential to be grateful whether you achieve success or not. If you are not there yet, it is about visualizing and imagining yourself to be successful.

Love your life no matter where you are on the ladder of success.

If you need to make changes, you should take every opportunity to do so with all your might.

You are reminded that you alone could make a success of your life.

Other people can be part of your success and happiness, but it is up to you to make it happen. Being successful does not mean that things are always easy, in any case. Stressful and competitive environments are everywhere, as sportspeople will attest to. We have mentioned LeBron James and Michael Jordan, who have had many successes but have also endured failure.

The corporate environment places high demands on executives as well. As with athletes, they need to be in an ideal performance state most of the time. In order for them to remain at the top of their game, they have to take care of themselves. It is recommended that the leaders improve their lives by taking care of their bodies, mental, spiritual, and emotional states. All of this can be achieved through meditation, which is a vital resource for a successful person. It covers a large part of any person's life and is not limited to specific religions or mindsets. Everyone can use it for his or her benefit.

One of the major partners of success is failure. This can only be true if you embrace it, turn it into a science, and overcome the fear of failure. Only then will you reap the benefits of success. Success comes with challenges, but Tzu has given us the keys to success as well. He stated the following in The Art of War:

"If you know the enemy and know yourself, you need not fear the result of a hundred battles. If you know yourself but not the enemy, for every victory gained you will also suffer a defeat. If you know neither the enemy nor yourself, you will succumb in every battle." Sun Tzu, The Art of War (Barker 2014).

Thus, successful people have specific characteristics that are built up over long periods. Athletes, for example, do not become successful overnight. It takes long hours of hard work and taking care of oneself. They form habits that sustain their high performance for more extended periods as well. You can also see from the practical examples of how this is accomplished.

We encourage you to make every effort to become the successful person that you endeavor to be. We take you through the steps to the point where you can take up the flag and carry it forward. In this book, we take you through the need to:

1. Find your own description of success
2. Give you the keys to success
3. Good Habits to be successful
4. See the secret habits of high-performance leaders
5. How high-performing leaders take care of self – "The Inner Man."
6. The impact of a positive mind-set and meditation on your life
7. Take practical steps to integrate meditation with success
8. Look at practical examples to guide and inspire you
9. See how successful people embrace failure as failure is an integral part of the success
10. To see failure from the science perspective
11. How to deal with the fear of failure
12. Know and understand your competitors and opponents
13. See how you can use technology in your meditation

-- [J.K.SIMON]

Check out Other Books

Go here to check out other related books that might interest you:

[**Note to freelancer:** Please ignore this. This chapter will be completed by myself.]
[**Note to self:** You can either omit this entire chapter or replace this with a list of 3-5 of:
a) Your other eBooks, or; b) Other graduates' eBooks, or; c) A mixture of your eBooks and other graduates' eBooks

Example:

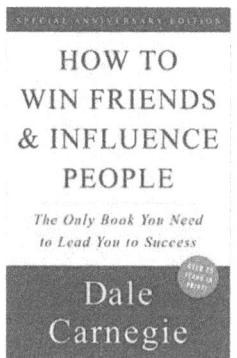

How To Win Friends and Influence People
http://www.amazon.com/dp/B003WEAI4E

How to Stop Worrying and Start Living
http://www.amazon.com/dp/B003WIYCCY

The Leader In You
http://www.amazon.com/dp/B003WIYCDI

Note to self: Remember to either delete this chapter or replace it with your own selection of eBooks]

References

Barker, Eric. "Sun Tzu's Art of War: How Ancient Strategy Can Lead to Modern Success." *Time*, Time, 2 June 2014, time.com/2801517/sun-tzus-art-of-war-how-ancient-strategy-can-lead-to-modern-success/.

Cooper, Belle Beth. "The Science of Failure: Why Highly Successful People Crave Mistakes." *Buffer Resources*, Buffer Resources, 30 June 2020, buffer.com/resources/why-highly-successful-people-crave-failure-and-mistakes/.

Gonzalez, Guadalupe. "Calm's Master Plan to Help the World Chill Out: Meet Stressed People Wherever They Are--and Bring Them LeBron James." *Inc.com*, Inc., 16 Dec. 2019, www.inc.com/guadalupe-gonzalez/calm-michael-acton-smith-alex-tew-company-year-nominee-2019.html.

Hayes, Julian. "3 Habits High Performing Leaders Must Commit to on a Daily Basis." *Inc.com*, Inc., 25 Apr. 2018, www.inc.com/julian-hayes-ii/3-essential-habits-of-high-performing-leaders.html.

Ho, Leon. "How To Be A Successful Person (And What Makes One Unsuccessful)." *Lifehack*, Lifehack, 6 Apr. 2020, www.lifehack.org/articles/productivity/these-are-the-things-that-make-successful-person-and-unsuccessful-person.html.

Kotobalavu, Kelera. "The Creative Process." *FijiTimes*, www.fijitimes.com/the-creative-process/.

Leamer, Nathan. "Fiji Rugby Wins Gold And Then Sings For The Glory of God!" *Medium*, Medium, 12 Aug. 2016, medium.com/@nathan_leamer/fiji-rugby-wins-gold-and-sings-for-the-glory-of-god-edb23125162a.

Loehr Jim and Tony Schwartz. "The Making of a Corporate Athlete." *Harvard Business Review*, 12 Feb. 2018, hbr.org/2001/01/the-making-of-a-corporate-athlete.

Poindexter, Cristina. "Mindful Technology Is on the Rise, but It's Time to Think beyond Meditation." *Medium*, Your Virtual Self, 3 Aug. 2018, medium.com/maslo/mindful-technology-is-on-the-rise-but-its-time-to-think-beyond-meditation-ce4d1de8e1c4.

Stasiulionyte, Inga. "10 Tips to Achieve Anything You Want in Life." *SUCCESS*, 17 Dec. 2019, www.success.com/10-tips-to-achieve-anything-you-want-in-life/.

The Mind Tools Content Team et al. "Overcoming Fear of Failure: Facing Fears and Moving Forward." *Don't Be Afraid of Failure From MindTools.com*, www.mindtools.com/pages/article/fear-of-failure.htm.

Titaniumsuccess. "Every Successful Person Embraces Failure." *Titanium Success*, Titanium Success, 30 Dec. 2019, titaniumsuccess.com/why-every-successful-person-embraces-failure/.

Ward, Marguerite. "9 Habits of Highly Successful People, from a Man Who Spent 5 Years Studying Them." *CNBC*, CNBC, 28 Mar. 2017, www.cnbc.com/2017/03/28/9-habits-of-highly-successful-people.html.

"What's the Secret Habit of High Performing Leaders?" *Get Lighthouse*, 26 Feb. 2018, getlighthouse.com/blog/high-performing-leaders-secret/.

White, Susan. "Positive Thinking Is the Key to Success: Benefits of Positive Thinking." *AllAssignmentHelp.com - Best Academic Helper US and Australia*, 26 Nov. 2019, www.allassignmenthelp.com/blog/positive-thinking-is-the-key-to-success/.

Wuest, Bob. *Upgrade Your Lifestyle: 10 Keys to Unlock a Steady State of Happiness*. Upgrade Your Lifestyle.com, 2018.

www.ingramcontent.com/pod-product-compliance
Lightning Source LLC
Chambersburg PA
CBHW070858050426
42453CB00012B/2267